Sarah's Surprise

Written by
Rob Waring and **Maurice Jamall**

Before You Read

put something in

to call someone

to drink (a drink)

to work

bag

café

cookies

food

husband and wife

ice cream

money

pants and shirt

police officer

sandwich (sandwiches)

surprised

In the story

Sarah

Ji-Sung

Mrs. Hayes

The man

"Hello, Sarah, I'm Mrs. Hayes," says a woman.
"How do you do, Mrs. Hayes?" says Sarah.
Mrs. Hayes has a café. The café's name is The Lagoon.
Sarah starts work at The Lagoon today.

Ji-Sung works at The Lagoon, too.
Mrs. Hayes says to him, "Ji-Sung, this is Sarah. She starts work today."
"Hi Sarah, it's nice to meet you. I'm Ji-Sung," he says.
"Hello, Ji-Sung," says Sarah. "Nice to meet you, too."

PITCH BLACK 4.00
LAGOON'S BREW 4.25
COFFEE W/ CREAM 4.50
EXPRESSO 5.00
COFFEE LATTE 5.50

CAPPUCCINOS
ICED CAPPUCCINO 5.50
MOCHACCINO 5.50

LAGOON'S SALAD 4.00
CAESAR SALAD 4.50
KING'S SALAD 5.00
NEPTUNE'S SALAD 6.50

CAKES
BELGIAN CAKE 3.00
CARROT CAKE 3.00
LEMON CAKE 3.00

ICE CREAM $1.99

Mrs. Hayes shows Sarah the things in the café.
She shows her the drinks and the food.
"This is the coffee maker," she says. "And this
is the ice-cream maker."
"Oh, okay," says Sarah.

Ji-Sung and Sarah are working in the café. A man and a woman come into the café.
The woman wants drinks and ice cream.
The man wants some cookies and some sandwiches.

Mrs. Hayes says, "Ji-Sung and Sarah, I'm going out now."
"Okay," says Sarah. "Bye."
Mrs. Hayes goes out.
Sarah and Ji-Sung work in the café.

A man comes into the café. He asks Sarah, "Hello. Is Janet here?"
Sarah says, "Janet? I'm sorry. I don't know Janet."
The man says, "Mrs. Hayes. Where is she?"
Sarah says, "Oh, Mrs. Hayes. She's shopping."
"Okay, thank you," says the man.

The man takes some sandwiches.
He puts them in his bag. He takes an apple, too.
Sarah watches him. She is surprised.
"What's the man doing?" she thinks. "Oh! He's
taking the sandwiches."
Ji-Sung does not see the man.

The man does not give the money to Sarah. He says nothing.
He walks out of the café with the food.
Sarah looks at the man. She is very surprised, but she says
nothing.
"What do I do?" she thinks.

"Ji-Sung! Ji-Sung! Come here!" she says.
Ji-Sung comes to Sarah. "Are you okay?" he asks.
Sarah tells Ji-Sung about the man.
"Oh, no," says Ji-Sung.
"What do we do?" Sarah asks.

Ji-Sung says, "Let's call the police."
Sarah calls the police. She tells the police officer about the man.
She says to the police officer, "Yes. Some sandwiches and an apple."
"Okay, thank you," says the police officer. "We are coming now."

A police officer comes to The Lagoon.
Sarah tells the police officer about the man.
"He is a big man," Sarah says. "He has a blue shirt
and white pants. He's about 45 years old."

Mrs. Hayes comes into the café. She sees the police officer.
"Hello, Sarah. Why are the police here?" she asks. "Is everything
okay?"
Sarah says, "No, Mrs. Hayes. Everything's *not* okay."
She tells Mrs. Hayes about the man.
"Oh, no," says Mrs. Hayes.

Sarah is talking with Mrs. Hayes and the police officer.
She sees the man. He is walking to the café.
"Mrs. Hayes, look! That's the man," says Sarah. "He's coming here!"
Sarah shows them the man. She says, "He has the sandwiches, Mrs. Hayes."

The man sees Mrs. Hayes.

"Is everything okay, Janet?" he asks. "Why are the police here?"

Mrs. Hayes says, "Sarah, this is my husband, Chris. This is *our* café."

She says, "He works near here. He gets his sandwiches here every day."

Sarah is very surprised. "Oh? He's your husband . . . !"

Goodbye, Hello!

Written by
Rob Waring and **Maurice Jamall**

to fall

birthday

brother

car

cart

class

shopping

sister

smile

snowboard

store

beautiful

little big

sad

Alex

Daniela

Jessica

Jenny

"Come on, Daniela. Let's go in here," says Alex.
Daniela and her brother Alex are shopping.
It is their mother's birthday on Thursday.
Alex and Daniela go into a big store.

Daniela looks at the CDs. "Look! It's here!" she says.
"What's here?" asks Alex.
Daniela says, "It's the CD by The Bandits."
"Oh, really?" says Alex, but he is not looking.

Alex is looking at the snowboards.

"Wow," he thinks. "I want *this* for my birthday!"

"Daniela, look at this," he says.

Daniela does not look. She is walking away.

A little girl is coming with a shopping cart.

The little girl is not looking. She does not see Alex.
"Look out!" says a man.
The girl hits Alex with the shopping cart.
"*Ouch*!" says Alex. He falls into the snowboards.

The snowboards fall onto Alex. "*Ouch*!" he says.
"Hey! What are you doing?"
He is very angry with the little girl.
The little girl says, "I'm sorry. Are you okay?"
"No, I'm not," he says.

A girl in red comes to them.
"Are you okay, Jessica?" she asks the little girl.
Jessica says, "I'm okay."
"Say sorry to the boy, Jessica!" says the girl.
"I'm sorry," says Jessica.
Alex looks at the girl in red. He thinks, "Wow!
She's very beautiful!"

"I'm sorry," says the beautiful girl. "Are . . . are you okay?"
Alex says, "Umm . . . Umm . . . I'm okay. I'm really okay,
thank you. Thank you!"
She looks at Alex. Alex looks at her. They smile.

The girl in red goes away.
"Goodbye," she says. She smiles
at Alex.
Alex looks at the girl. "Yeah,"
says Alex. "Bye."
He thinks, "I want to talk to her."
Alex looks at her. He thinks she is
very beautiful.
He thinks, "What's her name?"

Alex sees Daniela. "Daniela, what's that girl's name?" he asks.
"I don't know," she says. "Why?"
Alex says, "Oh, okay. Bye!"
"What? Alex! Where are you going?" she asks.
"Bye," he says. "I'm going now."
"But Alex . . . these bags . . . ," she says. "Don't go away!"
Alex does not listen. He wants to talk to the girl.

Alex goes out of the store. He sees the girl.
He thinks, "She's very beautiful. She's smiling at me."
Alex wants to talk to her.
"What's her name?" he thinks. "I like her, but does she like me?"
"I want to talk to her. I want to know her name," he thinks.

The girl's mother comes. Jessica gets into the car.
"Oh, no!" he thinks. "I don't know her name!"
"Oh no! She's going . . . ," he thinks. "She's going!"
The girl in red gets into the car.

Alex is sad, but the girl is smiling at him from the car.
The car goes away and Alex looks at her.
"She likes me!" he thinks. "But she's going! Oh no!"
He is happy, but he is sad.

Alex is in class. He is sad. He is thinking about the girl.
He wants to see her.
"Okay, everybody," says Mr. Williams. "Please listen."
But Alex does not listen to Mr. Williams.

"We have a new student today. This is Jenny Martin,"
says Mr. Williams.
Alex thinks, "It's the girl in red! She's in my class!"
The girl sees Alex and she comes to him.
She says, "Do you remember me?"
"Yes. And I remember your sister," he says smiling.
"Hello, I'm Alex."
She smiles and says, "I'm Jenny. Hello!"

Rain, Rain, Rain!

Written by
Rob Waring and **Maurice Jamall**

to fall off a bike

to get dressed

to get on a bike

to ride

to run

bus

clock

dog

gate

holiday

rain

train

cold

late

wet

Faye

Faye's mother

"Oh, no! It's Monday today. And I have school,"
thinks Faye.
She is looking at the rain. "I don't like the rain.
And it's raining today."
She thinks, "I don't want to go to school."

School starts at 9 o'clock. Now it's 8:20!
She looks at the clock.
"Oh no," she thinks. "I'm late for school!"
Faye gets dressed.

"Good morning, Faye," says her mother.

"Morning, Mom," she says.

Her mother says, "Please eat, Faye."

"Sorry, Mom, I'm late," says Faye.

"Late? Where are you going?" asks her mother.

"School," she says.

"But Faye . . . ," says her mother.
"Sorry, mom, I'm late. See you!" says Faye.
Faye's mother says, "But . . . , but . . ."
"Bye!" says Faye.
Faye runs out of the house.

Faye gets on her bike. Every day, Faye takes the train to school.
She rides to the train station on her bike.
She looks at her watch. She thinks, "I'm late. Oh, no! It's 8:35."
"And it's raining. I don't like the rain," she thinks.

The rain is coming down. Faye is getting wet.
A girl is walking a dog. Faye does not see the girl
and the dog.
"Look out," says the girl. Faye's bike hits the dog.
"I'm sorry," Faye says.
Faye falls off her bike. "Oh, no! My bike!" she says.

Faye gets up. "I'm very late," she thinks.

Faye pushes her bike to the station. She is cold and very wet.

She sees the station. She goes to the bike rack.

Faye puts her bike in the bike rack.
She looks at the clock. It's now 8:45.
"Good," she thinks. "The station is there."
Faye goes into the station.

BAYVIEW
STATION

BIKE RACK

"But where's the train?" she thinks.
A man says, "There are no trains today."
She sees a tree in front of the train.
"Oh no!" thinks Faye. "No trains today!"
She looks at her watch. It's now 8:47.

"What do I do?" she thinks. "School starts at 9 o'clock!"
Faye thinks, "How do I get to the school?"
She thinks, "Oh, the bus! The bus goes to the school!"
She runs to the bus station, but the bus is leaving.
"Wait for me!" she says. But the bus does not wait.

Faye waits for the next bus. She waits and waits.
There is no bus. "Where's the bus?" thinks Faye.
Faye does not see a car.
The car goes into the water. Now she is very very wet.

"Oh no! It is now 8:49," she thinks.
She runs to school. She's very cold and very wet.
A boy and girl are looking at Faye.
"Why is she running?" they think.

Faye runs and runs. She sees the school gate.
She thinks, "Good! There's the school."
She looks at her watch. It is 8:59.
"Good, I'm not late," she thinks.

Faye gets to school. She sees something on the school gate.
It says, "*No school today. School holiday.*"
"Oh no!" she thinks. "There's no school today."
"It's a school holiday. Oh no!" she says.

Bad Dog? Good Dog!

Written by
Rob Waring and **Maurice Jamall**

Before You Read

to hit

to take a dog for a walk

brother

dog

game

gate

meat

puppy

puppies

shopping

sister

store

street

bad

good

"Take this money, Yoon-Hee," says Mrs. Lee.
"Please go to the store with Ji-Sung."
Yoon-Hee and Ji-Sung are brother and sister.
But Ji-Sung says, "I don't want to do the shopping."
"Oh, come on, Ji-Sung," says Yoon-Hee. "Let's help Mom."

Yoon-Hee and Ji-Sung go out of the house. They walk to the store.

"I don't want to do the shopping," says Ji-Sung. "I want to play with my game."

But Yoon-Hee is not listening. She is looking at her paper.

"Eggs, meat, coffee, and milk," she says. "Come on, Ji-Sung!"

Yoon-Hee and Ji-Sung see their friend, Farina.
"Hi, Farina," says Yoon-Hee. "Do you want to come to the store with us?"
"Sorry, no. My dog Misha has puppies now," says Farina.
"Hello, puppies," says Yoon-Hee to the dogs.
A big dog comes over to them. His name is Dingo.

"Hi, Dingo. Come here!" says Yoon-Hee.

Farina says, "Dingo wants to go for a walk. I want to take him, but . . . ,"

"Come on, Dingo," says Yoon-Hee. "Come with us."

Dingo is happy. He wants to go with Yoon-Hee and Ji-Sung.

"Thank you," says Farina. "Thank you."

Yoon-Hee, Ji-Sung, and Dingo walk to the store.
Ji-Sung is not happy. "I don't want the dog. I don't like dogs."
Yoon-Hee is angry with her brother.
"We're taking Dingo for a walk. Farina is our friend," says
Yoon-Hee.
Ji-Sung is not listening. He is playing with his game.
Yoon-Hee says, "Okay. You and Dingo wait here. I'm going into
the store."

Yoon-Hee comes back. "I have the meat," she says. "Now you go and get the milk."

Ji-Sung says, "No, you get it. I don't want to go shopping."

Yoon-Hee is angry with Ji-Sung. He is not doing the shopping. "Okay. You and Dingo wait here," she says.

Ji-Sung is playing with his game. He is not listening to Yoon-Hee.

Yoon-Hee goes into the big store.
Ji-Sung waits with Dingo. He is playing with his game.
Dingo sees the meat. He looks at Ji-Sung. Ji-Sung is not
looking at Dingo.
Dingo wants the meat. He takes the meat.

Dingo runs down the street. Ji-Sung sees Dingo with the meat.
"Stop, Dingo!" says Ji-Sung.
Dingo looks at Ji-Sung, but he does not stop. Dingo runs away with the meat.
"Come here, Dingo!" says Ji-Sung. "Come here! You bad dog!"

Yoon-Hee comes out of the store. "Where's Dingo?" she asks.
"Over there," Ji-Sung says. "Sorry. He has the meat," he says.
"What? Dingo has the meat?" says Yoon-Hee. "Oh no!"
Yoon-Hee and her brother run after Dingo and the meat.

Yoon-Hee sees Dingo. "There he is," says Yoon-Hee.
"Where?" says Ji-Sung.
Yoon-Hee says, "He's there. He's at that fruit store."
Dingo is running to a woman. "Dingo, look out!" says Ji-Sung.
Dingo hits the woman.
"*Ouch*!" says the woman. She falls into the fruit.

"Dingo! Bad dog," says Yoon-Hee.
Yoon-Hee says to the woman, "I'm very sorry. Are you okay?"
Now Dingo is running into the street. He is not looking at the cars.
"Look out, Dingo!" says Ji-Sung.
"Come back!" says the man in the car. "Bad dog!" he says. "Come here!"

Dingo runs away. Yoon-Hee and Ji-Sung run after Dingo.
"Where is he now?" asks Ji-Sung.
Yoon-Hee says, "He's over there. Come on!"
Ji-Sung says, "Dingo! Come here!"
But Dingo runs and runs. Ji-Sung and Yoon-Hee run, too.

"Where's Dingo going?" asks Ji-Sung.
"He's going back to Farina's house," says Yoon-Hee. "He's at the gate."
Dingo jumps over the gate.
Yoon-Hee says, "Look. There's Farina."

Farina sees Yoon-Hee and Ji-Sung.
Dingo gives the meat to the puppies. They eat the meat.
Dingo is happy now.
"You are a very bad dog, Dingo," says Ji-Sung.
Yoon-Hee smiles. She says, "Yes, but you are a very good father!"

Get the Ball!

Written by
Rob Waring and **Maurice Jamall**

to fall		blue team	
to score a goal		red team	
to kick		referee	
to push		score	
to run		soccer	
		surprised	
bags		win	

In the story

Jenny

Kerry

Alex

Anthony

"I want the Blues to win," says Jenny. She is talking to her friend Kerry.
Today there is a big soccer game. The Reds are playing the Blues.
Kerry and Jenny are watching the game.
Kerry likes the Reds and Jenny likes the Blues.

Jenny's boyfriend Alex plays for the Blues.
Kerry likes Anthony. He plays for the Reds.
"Come on, the Blues," says Jenny. She wants the Blues
to win.
"Come on, the Reds," says Kerry.

It is a good game. Everybody wants the ball.
Alex is a good player. He takes the ball from Anthony.
"Alex is very good," says Jenny.
"He's okay," says Kerry. She does not like the Blues.

Alex has the ball. He kicks it at the Reds' goal.
Alex scores a goal for the Blues!
The score is 1–0 to the Blues.
Jenny says, "Good goal, Alex!"
Kerry says nothing. Kerry is not happy.

Anthony gets the ball, but Alex pushes him. Alex takes the ball.
The referee sees Alex.
"Hey!" says Anthony.
Kerry says, "Hey! Stop that, Alex."
Jenny says, "Good play, Alex!"

Anthony has the ball. He runs to the Blues' goal. Anthony scores a goal for the Reds!
"Good goal, Anthony!" says Kerry. Kerry is very happy.
Now the score is the Reds 1, the Blues 1.
But Jenny says nothing. Now she is not happy.

Alex looks at Anthony. He wants the Blues to win.
Anthony wants the Reds to win.
The two teams are having a good game.
"Come on, Anthony!" says Kerry. "Come on, the Reds."
"Come on, the Blues!" says Jenny. "Come on, Alex."

Anthony has the ball. He is running to the Blues goal.
Alex pushes Anthony. He takes the ball from Anthony.
"Hey!" says Kerry.
Anthony is angry with Alex. Anthony is a good player,
but he is not playing well now.
"Come on, Alex!" says Jenny.

Alex and Anthony run for the ball. But Alex kicks
Anthony and takes the ball.
"Ouch!" says Anthony. "Don't do that!"
Anthony is very angry with Alex now.
"Don't kick me!" he says.

Anthony is angry with Alex. He gets the ball
and kicks it away.
"Get the ball, Anthony," says Alex.
"No!" says Anthony.
Alex says, "Get the ball, Anthony!"
"No!" says Anthony. He is very angry with Alex.
"You get the ball, Alex!"

Anthony watches Alex get the ball.
But Anthony starts running. He runs at Alex.
Alex thinks, "Why is Anthony running at me?
What's he doing?"
Anthony says, "No, Alex. No!"

Anthony runs at Alex. "Alex!" he says.
Alex thinks, "Why is Anthony running at me?"
Anthony pushes Alex. Alex falls down. He is very surprised.
Alex says, "Hey! Anthony, what are you doing? Don't do that!"

"Look!" says Anthony.
"Look at what?" asks Alex. Some bags fall on the ball.
Anthony shows Alex the bags. "Look . . . the bags!
See!" says Anthony.
"Wow, Umm . . . Thanks!" says Alex.
"That's okay," says Anthony.

Everybody runs to Anthony and Alex. They are very
happy with Anthony.

"Alex! Alex, are you okay?" asks Jenny.

"I'm okay, thanks. Thanks, Anthony," says Alex.

"You're a good friend. Let's play soccer."

The Tickets

Written by
Rob Waring and **Maurice Jamall**

Before You Read

to fall

purse  bag

to hit

tickets

class

angry

lunch

hungry

lunchroom

late

money

surprised

In the story

Jenny

Jimmy

Kerry

Alex

"Happy birthday, Jenny!" says her friend Jimmy.
Today is Jenny's birthday.
"These are for you," he says. Jimmy gives Jenny
some tickets for her birthday.
"Wow! The tickets are for *The Bandits*. I love
them!" Jenny says. "Thank you, Jimmy."
Jimmy says, "There are two tickets. There's one
for you and one for Alex."
Alex is Jenny's boyfriend.

Jenny is very happy. Jenny's friend Kerry looks at the tickets.
"Wow!" she says. "When is it?"
Jimmy says, "It's on Saturday."
"Lucky you!" says Kerry. "I want to go!"
"But there are no more tickets," says Jimmy.

"But I really want to go," says Kerry. "Please give me a ticket, Jenny."

"Sorry," says Jenny. "These are *my* tickets. I'm going with Alex."

"Please?" asks Kerry. "I love *The Bandits,* but Alex doesn't like them."

Jenny and Jimmy are very surprised.

"No," says Jimmy. "They're Jenny's tickets. She wants to go with Alex."

Jimmy looks at the time. "Look, Jenny!" he says. "We're late for class."

"Okay, let's go!" says Jenny. "Are you coming, Kerry?"

Kerry says, "No, I don't have class now. See you at lunchtime."

"Bye!" they say.

Jimmy and Jenny go to class. They are really late.

Jimmy and Jenny go to the classroom.
A boy is running to class. He hits Jenny's bag.
"Oh, I'm sorry," he says.
"It's okay," says Jenny.
Something falls from Jenny's bag. Kerry sees it.
Jenny does not see it.
Jenny goes into the classroom.

Kerry sees Jenny's tickets. "What's that?" she thinks.
"Wow! These are Jenny's tickets!"
Kerry looks at the tickets, "I want to go, but they are
not *my* tickets. They are Jenny's."
"Jenny's in her class now, but we are meeting at
lunchtime," she thinks. She puts the tickets in her purse.

In class, Jenny says, "Alex, I want to show you something."
She looks in her bag for the tickets. They are not there.
Jenny says to Jimmy, "Jimmy! The tickets! Where are the
tickets? They're not in my bag!"
"Oh no!" says Jimmy. "Where are they?"

It is lunchtime. Kerry is waiting for Jenny and Jimmy. Jenny's tickets are in Kerry's purse. She wants to give the tickets to Jenny.

Kerry thinks, "Where is Jenny? I have her tickets."

But Jenny does not come.

Jimmy comes to the lunchroom.

"Hi, Jimmy," says Kerry.

"Hi, let's have lunch. I'm very hungry," says Jimmy.

"Where's Jenny?" asks Kerry. "I have something for her."

Jimmy says, "She's coming, Kerry. Let's eat. I'm really hungry."

"Okay," she says.

Kerry gets a sandwich. She opens her purse. She takes out some money.

Jimmy sees Jenny's tickets in Kerry's purse. He is very surprised. Jimmy thinks, "Why does Kerry have Jenny's tickets?"

He thinks, "Oh, I know! Kerry wants the tickets. She wants to go to the concert. That's really bad!"

Jimmy is angry with Kerry. "Kerry, that's very bad," says Jimmy.
"Excuse me?" says Kerry. She is very surprised.
"Jenny's your friend!" says Jimmy.
"Yes, Jenny's my friend," she says.

Jimmy says, "But you're *not* a good friend!"
Jimmy is thinking about Jenny's tickets. They are in Kerry's purse.
"What are you saying?" says Kerry. "I don't understand."
Jimmy says, "That's really bad of you."
"Jimmy, what are you talking about?" asks Kerry.

Jenny comes into the lunchroom. Kerry and Jimmy see Jenny.

"Oh! Jenny! Here are your tickets," says Kerry.

Kerry tells Jenny about the tickets.

"Thanks, Kerry," says Jenny. "That's very nice of you."

Jimmy thinks, "Oh no! Kerry *doesn't* want the tickets. She's a *good* friend."

Jimmy is very surprised. Jenny shows the tickets to Alex.
Kerry asks, "Jimmy, why are you angry with me? I don't
understand."
"I'm sorry. It's okay. It's nothing!" he says.
Kerry looks at Jimmy. "Nothing?"
Jimmy's face is very red. "Yes, nothing."